Air,
Boat,
Road

T0381966

Written by Natasha Paul
Illustrated by Joe Bucco

Collins

hot air balloon

2

rocket is higher

hot air balloon

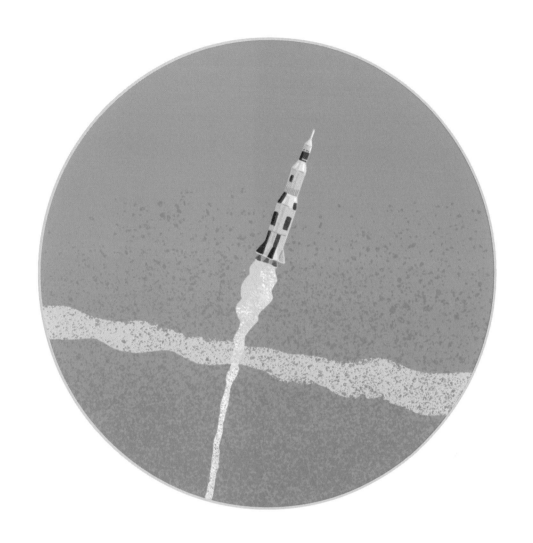

rocket is higher

pair of boats

lights shimmer

pair of boats

lights shimmer

digger

pink car is the winner

11

digger

pink car is the winner

 Review: After reading

Use your assessment from hearing the children read to choose any GPCs, words or tricky words that need additional practice.

Read 1: Decoding

- Use grapheme cards to make any words you need to practise. Model reading those words, using teacher-led blending.
- Ask the children to follow as you read the whole book, demonstrating fluency and prosody.

Read 2: Vocabulary

- Look back through the book and discuss the pictures. Encourage the children to talk about details that stand out for them. Use a dialogic talk model to expand on their ideas and recast them in full sentences as naturally as possible.
- Work together to expand vocabulary by naming objects in the pictures that children do not know.
- Look at pages 8 and 9 and ask: Which word tells us that there are two boats that look the same? (*pair*) Which word describes the ship's lights? (*shimmer*) Discuss its meaning and what else might shimmer. (e.g. *sparkle, sunlight on a lake*)

Read 3: Comprehension

- Ask the children what type of road, air or boat ride they would enjoy most, and why.
- Discuss what the children have found out from the book using pages 14 and 15 as a prompt. For example, ask: What sort of balloon is this? (*hot air balloon*) What goes higher than a hot air balloon? (*rocket*) What won a race? (*the pink car*)